UNDERSTANDING
SIKHISM

BY MICHAEL REGAN

CONTENT CONSULTANT

Pashaura Singh

Chair, Department of Religious Studies
Professor and Saini Chair in Sikh Studies
University of California, Riverside

Essential Library

An Imprint of Abdo Publishing | abdopublishing.com

UNDERSTANDING
WORLD RELIGIONS
AND BELIEFS

ABDOPUBLISHING.COM

Published by Abdo Publishing, a division of ABDO, PO Box 398166, Minneapolis, Minnesota 55439. Copyright © 2019 by Abdo Consulting Group, Inc. International copyrights reserved in all countries. No part of this book may be reproduced in any form without written permission from the publisher. Essential Library™ is a trademark and logo of Abdo Publishing.

Printed in the United States of America, North Mankato, Minnesota
022018
092018

Cover Photo: Shutterstock Images
Interior Photos: Chicco Dodi FC/Shutterstock Images, 4–5, 12; Sylvie Jarrossay/Alamy, 8; A. Katz/Shutterstock Images, 10–11; Shutterstock Images, 15 (left), 15 (right), 23, 25, 73, 94, 96–97; David Longstreath/AP Images, 16–17; Dima Fadeev/Shutterstock Images, 18; Viktorija Reuta/Shutterstock Images, 20; Bebeto Matthews/AP Images, 21; Yvan Travert/akg-images/Newscom, 26–27, 28, 46–47; Rahmat Gul/AP Images, 30; Art Directors & Trip/ArkReligion.com/Alamy, 32, 42, 45; DR Travel Photo and Video/Shutterstock Images, 35; Paul Fearn/Alamy, 36–37; Tukaram Karve/Shutterstock Images, 38; Fayaz Kabli/Reuters/Newscom, 40; Christine Osborne/ World Religions Photo Library/Alamy, 48; AP Images, 54; World History Archive/Newscom, 56–57; The Print Collector Heritage Images/ Newscom, 58; Patrick Doyle/Reuters/Newscom, 61; Colin McConnell/Toronto Star/Getty Images, 65; Pacific Press/Sipa USA/Newscom, 66–67, 78–79; Iryna Rasko/Shutterstock Images, 68; Tim Page/Eye Ubiquitous/Alamy, 71; Hindustan Times/Rex Features/AP Images, 74–75; Aleksandar Todorovic/Shutterstock Images, 76–77; John Gress/Reuters/Newscom, 82–83; Chris Maddaloni/CQ Roll Call/AP Images, 84; Faisal Mahmood/Reuters/Newscom, 86–87; Elena Mirage/Shutterstock Images, 88; Jayanta Shaw/Reuters/Newscom, 91; Sipra Das/The India Today Group/Getty Images, 93

Editor: Claire Vanden Branden
Series Designer: Maggie Villaume

LIBRARY OF CONGRESS CONTROL NUMBER: 2017961414

PUBLISHER'S CATALOGING-IN-PUBLICATION DATA

Name: Regan, Michael, author.
Title: Understanding Sikhism / by Michael Regan.
Description: Minneapolis, Minnesota : Abdo Publishing, 2019. | Series: Understanding world religions and beliefs | Includes online resources and index.
Identifiers: ISBN 9781532114298 (lib.bdg.) | ISBN 9781532154126 (ebook)
Subjects: LCSH: Sikhism--Doctrines--Juvenile literature. | Spiritual life--Sikhism--Juvenile literature. | World religions--Juvenile literature. | Religious belief--Juvenile literature.
Classification: DDC 294.6--dc23

CONTENTS

BAISAKHI FESTIVAL

A Sikh family in Punjab, India, excitedly awakened early on the morning of Baisakhi. The April festival is a celebration of the tenth guru's establishment of a holy order of warriors. The family quickly bathed and then dressed in their new, brightly colored clothes. On this day of celebrating the holy scriptures and the beginnings of their Sikh identity, they set off for the gurdwara, or local temple, to begin the day's activities. Once there, they all participated in the special prayer meeting. At the end of the prayers, each family member received *karah prasad*, a special sweet treat, before beginning the *langar*, or community lunch, provided in the temple dining hall.

Next the family rushed outside to get the best view of the *nagar kirtan*, a special Baisakhi procession accompanied by the singing of hymns. Loud, joyous singing and music reached their ears before they saw five men dressed in bright orange outfits and turbans.

Many Sikhs attended the Baisakhi festival in Vicenza, Italy, in 2017.

THE DANCES
FOR BAISAKHI

Two folk dances are typically performed during Baisakhi celebrations. Women perform one dance, called the *gidda* or *giddha*. Men perform the other, called the *bhangra*.

The gidda, which arose from the harvest times of Punjab, is a vigorous dance that includes graceful movement of the feet and arms. The music is provided by singers, clapping, and the constant beat of the *dhol*, a double-headed drum. Dancers wear colorful outfits during the joyful presentation.

The bhangra originally expressed everyday farming scenes. It originated in the Punjab regions of what are now India and Pakistan. The bhangra is a very physically demanding dance with lots of leaps and bending. This dance is also accompanied by the beat of a dhol. Today, the bhangra has been incorporated into popular music styles, such as the disco, reggae, and rap of other countries, particularly in the United Kingdom.

These impressive-looking bearded men led the procession carrying big swords like their ancestors.

Following close behind came brightly dressed singers and dancers of all ages. Martial arts experts demonstrated moves in mock duels. Drummers and musicians played their instruments to the delight and entertainment of both watchers and participants. A colorfully decorated open truck transported the Sikh holy scriptures along the parade route.

After the procession passed, the family set off for the festival site. Like at fairs worldwide, the family feasted on tasty foods at the festival site. They visited booths selling Sikh art, clothing, and jewelry. Musicians and dancers were everywhere. Demonstrations of Sikh wrestling and crafts intrigued the family. People gathered in the area of worship. The langar meal was provided for all

SIKH MUSICAL INSTRUMENTS

Sikh musical instruments were originally used for accompanying *kirtan*, the singing of sacred scriptures. During kirtan, a variety of instruments can be used. There are two main types of instruments. The first type is *svaravad*, or note instruments. The other type is *tal vad*, or rhythm instruments.

Examples of the svaravad are the *rabab*, *sitar*, *sarod*, and *bansari*. These are stringed instruments that are shaped similarly to violins, guitars, and violas. Another note instrument is the harmonium. It is a small organ that is powered by air from a bellows. The player uses one hand to work the bellows and the other hand to play the keyboard notes. People describe it as sounding like an accordion.

The tal vad instruments include the tabla, a set of two drums, and the mridanga, a longer, single drum. Small cymbals are also used as instruments. The most common combination of instruments used today during kirtan are the harmonium, the tabla, and some cymbals. Many traditional Sikh instruments continue to take their place in daily devotional activities, which happen either in the temple or at home.

attendees. In the farming areas of Punjab, other Sikh families were celebrating the harvest season in addition to the religiously important Baisakhi festival. They also had singing and dancing. At the end of the day, all the families returned to their homes for final prayers and bedtime.

Traditional folk dances are performed at the Baisakhi festival every year.

Why Celebrate?

Baisakhi originally started in the farming areas of Punjab as a thanksgiving for a bountiful harvest and a prayer for the following year's plantings. Sikhs also celebrate Baisakhi for a number of important religious reasons. Baisakhi commemorates the day in 1699 when the tenth guru of the Sikhs, Gobind Singh, founded the Khalsa Sikhs, an order of religious warriors. On this day he also initiated five followers called the *panj pyare*, or five beloved, with a special ceremony. The ceremony, called *Amrit Sanskar*, became the initiation into the Khalsa Sikhs. This was part of the beginning of a national identity for the Sikhs in India. Most outsiders in modern times think of this identity and its traditions when they think about Sikhs today. However, it is important to know that not all Sikhs are Khalsa. Other sects, or groups of Sikhs, exist within Sikhism.

This day is also celebrated as the time when Guru Gobind Singh announced that he would be the last human guru, or teacher, of the Sikhs. The word *guru* has been explained as one who dispels ignorance, *gu*, and brings enlightenment, *ru*. Guru Gobind Singh then said that the holy scriptures of Sikhism would be the guru after his death. The book called Guru Granth Sahib is considered a living being. The name means "Honorable Guru in book form."[1] A copy of the Guru Granth Sahib is kept in all Sikh temples throughout the world.

Every year during the nagar kirtan, Sikhs sweep the street to make it clean for the passing of the Guru Gobind Singh.

Baisakhi Worldwide

Ninety percent of all Sikhs worldwide live in India. The 22 million Sikhs living there make Sikhism the fourth-largest religion in India. Approximately 2.5 million more Sikhs live elsewhere in the world.[2]

Canada has the second-largest population of Sikhs in the world. Most of the nation's 455,000 Sikhs live in the province of British Columbia on Canada's west coast.[3] The town of Surrey in British Columbia has the largest Baisakhi celebration outside of India. In 2015, it was estimated that more than 250,000 people participated in the parade.[4] Anyone is free to join in the festivities, which emphasize Sikh values of equality and community-based living.

A large number of Sikhs also live in the United Kingdom, particularly in Birmingham and London. The United Kingdom has the third-largest population of Sikhs in the world. As of early 2017, approximately 430,000 Sikhs were living in the

GURU GRANTH SAHIB

Guru Granth Sahib is considered the Word of Waheguru, which means God in the Punjabi language, as revealed to six of the ten Sikh gurus and other saints of Sikhism. Sikhs believe the scriptures are the actual words and verses spoken by the gurus.

Guru Granth Sahib is written in the Punjabi language. It contains almost 6,000 hymns in its 1,430 pages. The scriptures were written down and added to until the tenth guru, Gobind Singh, declared the book complete and then instilled it with life. Guru Granth Sahib is considered a living being and is respected as such.

United Kingdom.[5] Because of this, Baisakhi celebrations have become hugely popular there. The festival is attended by Sikhs and non-Sikhs.

There is no US government census data on Sikhs in the United States, but it is estimated that approximately 250,000 to 500,000 lived in the United States as of early 2017, according to the Sikh Coalition.[6] Estimates of the Sikh populations of Kenya, Uganda, and Tanzania indicate between 50,000 and 100,000 Sikhs live in East Africa. Several other countries have significant numbers of Sikhs. Malaysia and Bangladesh both have Sikh populations of 100,000. Australia, Italy, and Thailand are each the home to approximately 70,000 Sikhs.[7]

TRADITIONAL SIKH CLOTHES

Bana, the traditional Sikh spiritual clothing, can be colorful for both women and men. Bright yellows, blues, oranges, pinks, purples, and other hues are worn by both sexes. Turbans are seen on practically all men, and some women wear them too.

The most recent Sikh code of conduct, which dates from 1931, requires men to wear both a turban and a loose undergarment called a *kachhera*. For Sikh men in general, traditional clothing includes the kurta pajama. The kurta is a long shirt that reaches from mid-thigh to the knees. This is worn over a loose pair of pants, called the pajama. The shirt and pants can be of any color and pattern for festive occasions. More devout Sikhs typically wear simpler styles with solid colors to display humility. Sikh warriors traditionally wear a *chola*. It is a type of robe with long panels that allow for freedom of movement when the warrior is involved in combat.

A Sikh man and woman dressed in
traditional clothing

Traditional clothing for women includes the *salwar kameez*. The salwar are baggy, loose-fitting pants with ankle cuffs. These are topped by the kameez, which is a dress top. These clothes come in many colors and patterns and are often decorated with embroidery. Similar to the men, devout women tend to wear simple prints or solid colors without decorations as a sign of humility.

WHAT IS SIKHISM?

Sikhism was founded more than 500 years ago. Guru Nanak Dev began the religion in the Punjab district, which is now in India and Pakistan. Guru Nanak was born in Punjab to parents who followed the Hindu faith. Hinduism was the major religion in India at the start of Sikhism.

The Sikh religion is based upon the teachings of Guru Nanak and the nine Sikh gurus who succeeded him. As of April 2017, Sikhism had more than 24 million followers, making it the fifth-largest religion in the world.[1] The name *Sikh* in the Punjabi language means "learner" or "disciple." Those who join the Sikh religion are seeking to learn from the spiritual guidance provided by the gurus.

Guru Nanak and the nine gurus who came after him provided the spiritual guidance of the Sikhs. Today, the holy teachings contained in the Guru Granth Sahib guide the Sikhs' daily life.

Sikhism is among the newest of the world's largest religions.

Sikhs value time with God above all other practices.

Sikh Beliefs

The Sikhs believe there is only one supreme being, or God. They refer to God as Waheguru. To them, the God of their religion is the same God as that of all other religions. For example, the Sikh God is the same one that Muslims and Christians worship.

VISITING A GURDWARA

When a person visits a gurdwara there are some things to remember. Gurdwaras are open to people of all religions. But before entering, shoes should be removed. Feet and hands should be washed if they are dirty. Upon entering, each person's head must be covered. Many gurdwaras provide a head covering of some kind if a visitor does not have one.

In the main prayer hall is a copy of the Guru Granth Sahib. There are no benches or chairs, so visitors either stand, kneel, or sit cross-legged on the floor. It is important when sitting during worship that visitors not point their feet in the direction of the holy book or turn their back on it because those are signs of disrespect.

A holy offering, called karah prasad, is provided to everyone entering a gurdwara. It is a small sweet made of butter, sugar, and flour. It should be accepted with cupped hands and eaten with the right hand. It is considered disrespectful to refuse it or throw it away.

Sikhs believe all people are equal. To Sikhs, all religions, ethnic groups, and castes are equal in the eyes of God and are to be treated as such. Men and women are also fully equal in Sikhism.

Remembering God on a daily basis is important to Sikhs. They believe a person should keep God in mind at all times. However, this inner remembrance is not brought about by rituals. The first Sikh guru rejected all forms of ritual that other religions practiced. Worshiping statues, going on long pilgrimages, and fasting were some rituals the Sikhs did not originally consider to be of high importance. The first Sikh guru, Guru Nanak, rejected these sorts of rituals as he believed they were a distraction from the God inside each human heart. However, they are not forbidden practices. In fact, many Sikhs have adopted the practice of making a pilgrimage to the historic gurdwara, Harmandir Sahib, in India. It is also called the Golden Temple because the upper part was covered in gold when it was rebuilt in the early 1800s after it was damaged in an attack. Along with this,

SIKH SYMBOL

Just as Christianity has a cross and Judaism has the Star of David, Sikhism has an emblem called the khanda to symbolize its faith. The khanda is made up of three symbols combined. There is the Chakkar, an inner circle that symbolizes the perfection of God with no beginning or end. It also represents a cooking pot and the sharing of food with the community. Two kirpans, or curved swords, on the outside symbolize the guru's spiritual and worldly leadership. A central two-edged sword symbolizes divine knowledge, with its sharp edges separating truth from lies.

Sikhs believe in religious freedom. To them, all people have the right to practice their religion as they wish.

Sikhs also believe it is extremely important to actively do good works in addition to daily devotions and meditations. Guru Nanak criticized detaching oneself from the world to only pray and meditate. Sikhism teaches that a person's main task is being fully involved in life by providing for one's family and helping the poor, the oppressed, and those in need. The Sikhs have a long history of standing up for those who cannot defend themselves and speaking out against injustice.

Sikhs have small versions of the Guru Granth Sahib that they can carry around with them.

Sikh Rehat Maryada

The Sikh Rehat Maryada is the code of conduct or way of life for Sikhs. It provides the official description of who is a Sikh. The official definition says that any man or woman who believes in one God is a Sikh. A belief in Guru Granth Sahib and the words and teaching of the ten gurus is also required. The final characteristic of a Sikh is belief in the Amrit Sanskar, or initiation, started by the tenth guru. A Sikh also must not belong to another religion.

The Sikhs believe salvation comes through a union with God. This union with God comes through love by realizing God dwells within a person's own being. They also believe that oneness with God cannot occur until a person has conquered the five thieves, or sins: lust, anger, greed, materialism, and pride. Sikhs believe that separation from God is what causes human suffering. If one becomes separate from God, life is not affirmed. They believe that grace from God is needed for oneness. However, a person cannot be one with God solely by good behavior.

Creation and Afterlife

The Sikhs believe that only God knows how and when the world came to be. Sikhs don't believe this is essential information to understanding God. Sikhs also see death as a very natural part of the life cycle. But Sikhism mostly focuses on how to act in this life and emphasizes being one with God. People can meditate and focus on loving God in order to get closer to salvation. Sikhs believe that when a person dies, he or she continues to die and come back to life until that person is right with God. Once that cycle ends, a person's soul lives on forever as part of God.

Sikh Daily Music

To the Sikhs, singing the sacred scriptural hymns is a way of spiritual communication with God. This is called *shabad kirtan*, or singing the praises of God. The morning prayers in the gurdwaras and the evening hymns sung at home are ways of developing the spiritual side of a person. These rituals also show devotion to the Timeless Being, or God. In Sikh temples, the *granthi*, or appointed reader of the sacred texts, may sing the hymns. Also, trained Sikh musicians, called *ragis*, will sing. The purpose of hearing, remembering, and singing the praises of God is so Sikhs remember the name of God throughout their daily lives.

A Sikh woman plays music during the nagar kirtan in 2017 in Secunderabad, India.

SIKHISM SUPPORTS ENVIRONMENTALISM

The Sikhs' environmental focus fits well with their ideals of service to the community and the well-being of all. Dr. Susan Prill is an associate professor of religion at Juanita College in Pennsylvania. In 2015, she published an article on the Sikhs' style of environmentalism. She wrote, "Like many religious communities, Sikhism is increasingly grappling with ways of responding to the global environmental crisis."[2] Going back to Sikhism's earliest beginnings, her research suggests several of the Sikh gurus saw care for the environment as a vital part of their faith.

Sikh "green works" take many forms. One form is community litter cleanup during a green nagar kirtan. Another way is through encouraging tree planting. This often takes place around the planet on Sikh Environment Day, which happens on March 14. The environmental organization EcoSikh provides guidelines on the use of biodegradable plates during free meals at Sikh temples, holy days, and festivals.

Sikhs believe that humans and the environment are equally important, so both should be treated with respect.

A Sikh charitable hospital in Punjab called Pingalwara established a farm using techniques for making natural fertilizers and other sustainable farming practices. All of these activities contribute to the "greening" of Sikhism that benefits individuals and the global community.

THE FIRST FOUR GURUS OF SIKHISM

Sikhism started around 1499. India and its largely Hindu population had been under the domination of the Delhi Sultanate for more than 300 years. It was an unsettled time in the country. The Delhi Sultanate conquerors were Muslims from Afghanistan. But the Sultanate was losing control to the Mughals. The Mughals, who were also Muslims, came from directly north of India. The Mughals gained full control of northern India during the lifetime of the founder of Sikhism and the first Sikh guru, Guru Nanak Dev Ji.

The First Sikh Guru

Guru Nanak was born in 1469 in the town of Nankana Sahib in the Punjab region. He was a member of the Hindu caste that specialized

Sikh women honor Guru Nanak Dev Ji during a celebration by carrying his portrait.

in accounting. After schooling and marriage, he became a storekeeper.

In his late twenties, Guru Nanak had an overwhelming religious experience. It began as he was taking a bath in a stream. He disappeared for three days and was thought to have drowned. But upon his return, Guru Nanak said he had been taken up by God and was told there was no distinction, in God's eyes, between Hindus and Muslims. Nanak said God gave him a cup of nectar and told him to drink from it. In God's name, Nanak was told to "rejoice in my name and teach others to do so."[1] With this, Nanak began his religious journey.

An illustration depicts Guru Nanak after he emerged from his religious experience in the stream.

When he returned from his experience, Guru Nanak quit his job, left Punjab, and traveled for 20 years to talk about what he had learned. Guru Nanak reportedly made five journeys. He first traveled throughout eastern India. Then he went south to present-day Sri Lanka, an island off the southern coast of India. His third journey took him to the Himalayan mountains in the north. His trip to the west took him to Baghdad, Mecca, and Medina in present-day Iraq and Saudi Arabia. His final journey was around Punjab itself.

GURU NANAK'S FRIEND

As Guru Nanak traveled across southern Asia for approximately 20 years, he was accompanied by his best friend, Bhai Mardana. Mardana was an expert musician. Mardana would play his *rabab*, a stringed instrument, while the guru sang his message of love and unity. Thus began the Sikh practice of spiritual music, which is now one of the foundations of the Sikh faith.

Throughout his journeys, Guru Nanak spread word of his spiritual insights by singing poems he had composed. Upon his return to Nankana Sahib, he founded a community of followers who lived together and worshiped on a daily basis. This place was called Kartarpur. The community was first made up of people from the caste of traders and merchants. Later, members of the peasant and rural landowner caste flocked to Sikhism. It was there in Kartarpur that the Sikh religion took hold.

Sikh students in Afghanistan attend school at a local gurdwara. Guru Angad cared deeply about providing education to Sikh children.

The Second Guru: Angad

Before Guru Nanak died in 1539, he appointed a formerly Hindu man as his successor. Guru Angad, whose Hindu name was Bhai Lehna, had been passing by Kartarpur while leading a pilgrimage and was enchanted by a man reciting Guru Nanak's hymns. He asked to meet Guru Nanak and immediately renounced his Hindu faith and started following the teachings of the first Sikh guru. He was a loyal and obedient follower of Guru Nanak and, after seven years, was appointed to be Guru Nanak's successor.

Guru Angad continued Guru Nanak's work. He created many Sikh schools and made langar a requirement in all the Sikh gurdwaras. During his 13 years as guru, he helped Sikhism become an accepted faith in India. Before his death in 1552, he appointed Amar Das as his successor. All of the gurus appointed their successor before they died.

INDIA'S CASTE SYSTEM

The caste system in India comes from the Hindu religion. The system was justified in its earliest times as necessary to ensure the order and security of society. The system is thought to be more than 3,000 years old. The caste system divided Hindus into a very strict ranking of groups. Typically, the higher castes were given more respect and wealth. These different groups were based on what people did for work. The highest caste contained teachers and priests. These people were called Brahmins. The next caste, the Kshatriyas, were warriors and rulers. The third caste included farmers, traders, and merchants, called Vaishyas. The next-lowest caste included laborers called Shudras. There was an even lower caste that was so low that its members were called Outcastes or Dalits. These people were street sweepers and latrine cleaners. Although Sikhism asserted that all people were equal, the Sikhs were mostly people in the Vaishya caste.

WISE AND HUMBLE

Guru Angad was said to be a wise and humble man. Other holy men and political leaders sought his blessings and wanted to engage him in spiritual conversations. A Mughal emperor, Humayun, had been recently defeated in battle by a Delhi Sultanate army in southern India. The deposed emperor was passing through Guru Angad's town on his retreat out of India. Humayun stopped to gain the guru's blessing but had to wait because the guru was singing religious hymns. The Mughal leader became impatient and was about to draw his sword when the guru responded. He commented on Humayun's recent defeat, "When you should have used the sword you did not, rather you ran away from the battlefield like a coward. Here you show off, threatening to attack unarmed devotees engaged in prayer."[2] Humayun asked forgiveness and was blessed by the guru. Eventually, the Mughal leader regained his throne.

The Third Teacher: Guru Amar Das

The third guru of the Sikhs was also a converted Hindu man. Like his immediate predecessor, Guru Amar Das was captivated by one of Guru Nanak's hymns, which he heard while passing by on a pilgrimage to the Ganges River. Guru Amar Das took over guidance of the panth, or Sikh community, when he was 73 years old. He guided the Sikhs to the new township of Goindwal, which was a short distance from Kartarpur. The new town was paid for by a wealthy supporter of Guru Angad.

Guru Amar Das's role as spiritual leader began more than 30 years after Guru Nanak started Sikhism. The original excitement about the religion was starting to wear off. In order to solidify their faith, he decreed that followers observe several rituals, such as a pilgrimage to a sacred well that was dug for that purpose.

The Sikhs were also spreading out from their original community of Kartarpur to all of Punjab. Guru Amar Das created administrative areas around the Punjab region to help coordinate the spread of Sikhism and

Guru Amar Das served as guru for 22 years.

organize the faithful. Sikhism's primary focus on the internal connection to God remained despite the changes made by the third guru.

Guru Ram Das: The Fourth Guru

In 1574, around the age of 40, Ram Das became the fourth guru of the Sikhs. He was the son-in-law of Guru Amar Das. He is best known for founding the city of Amritsar. Now located in India, this city became the capital of the Sikh religion. It is also the location of the Sikhs' holiest gurdwara, the Golden Temple.

In the late 1570s, the Sikhs moved their center of power to Amritsar. It is located northwest of New Delhi, India, and east of Lahore, Pakistan. At this time, many of the previous inhabitants of the land started joining the Sikhs. These people, the Jats, had been nomadic animal herders in the 1100s but had settled in the area to become farmers. The Jats had a tradition of defying authority. This tradition would later have an impact on the future of the Sikhs because of the Jats' willingness to fight back against oppression.

Guru Ram Das started the new tradition of establishing separate *masands*, or religions leaders, for individual congregations. This allowed for more personal contact with the Sikh panth. The masands, representatives of the guru, would present reports and bring gifts to the guru at least once a year. Guru Ram Das then appointed his son Arjan as his successor. All of the following gurus of Sikhism would be direct descendants of Ram Das.

The Golden Temple in Amritsar is surrounded by a sacred body of water called the Amrit Sarovar, which means "pool of nectar."

THE MILITANT GURUS

The Sikhs turned from relatively peaceful devotees of their religion in the 1600s to fierce fighters by the 1700s. This change came about because of the martyrdom of the fifth and ninth gurus. Their successors, the sixth and tenth gurus, took strong actions to arm the Sikhs against any threatening forces.

A Martyr: Guru Arjan

Guru Arjan was only 18 years old when he became the fifth guru of Sikhism in 1581. His oldest brother, Prithi Chand, did not take kindly to being passed over by his father, Ram Das. Later, Chand tried but failed to poison Arjan's only son, Hargobind. Chand and his followers also passed around unauthorized hymns that they said were written by earlier gurus. To combat this, Guru Arjan put together the real

Guru Arjan believed Sikhs should be generous and give 10 percent of their incomes to charities.

On special occasions and holidays, the Adi Granth is read from start to finish without stopping. The entire reading takes around 48 hours.

hymns in a book called the Adi Granth. With some additions, the Adi Granth would later become Guru Granth Sahib.

The panth grew steadily under Guru Arjan. For a while, things were peaceful for the Sikhs. Even when the Muslim Mughals conquered most of India in the late 1500s, the Sikhs went untouched.

The Mughal emperor Akbar was very tolerant of non-Islamic religions. However, that changed quickly after Akbar died in 1605 and his son, Jahangir, became the new emperor. At this time, Sikhism was attracting thousands of Hindus and Muslims. Jahangir saw the Sikhs as a threat to the Mughals. The new hostility by the Mughals eventually led to the execution in 1606 of the fifth Sikh guru, Guru Arjan, when he refused to quit preaching. Aware of growing hostility toward the Sikhs, Guru Arjan had urged his son, Hargobind, the next guru, to always carry arms.

Guru Hargobind: Spiritual and Civic Leader

The hostile situation with the Mughals did not improve under the sixth guru, Guru Hargobind. Following the orders of his father, Guru Hargobind instituted *miri/piri*, which means temporal authority/spiritual authority. Guru Hargobind became a mir, the civic leader of his people, in addition to being a pir, their spiritual leader.

Over the next 200 years, the Sikhs moved from being a mostly peaceful people to being fearless fighters against their oppressors.

THE ADI GRANTH

The Adi Granth is the first version of the Sikh holy scriptures. The fifth guru of the Sikhs, Arjan, collected and wrote down his own hymns and those of the previous gurus, Nanak, Angad, Amar Das, and Ram Das, in 1604. He also included in the book some songs of saints from both the Hindu and Islamic religions. One hundred years later, Guru Gobind Singh, the last human Sikh guru, added hymns created by his predecessor Guru Tegh Bahadur.

Hargobind's birthday is celebrated every year on July 5. During these celebrations, priests hand out food to fellow Sikhs.

The Sikhs officially rejected Mughal rule and stated that the guru was now both the civic and religious ruler. The Mughals were upset with this. Hargobind was considered a great military leader by his people. He fought four skirmishes with the Mughals and defeated them each time. Despite that, the Mughals forced the Sikhs out of Amritsar, southeast across the plains of Punjab, to the foothills of the Himalayan mountains.

There, the Sikhs established the new cities of Kiratpur and Anandpur in the mid-1600s. This land was under the control of the Hindus, so the Sikhs had some relief from the Mughals. The Sikhs lived in relative peace for approximately 60 years. There Hargobind remained until his death in 1644. He named his grandson Har Rai to be his successor.

The Seventh Guru: Har Rai

Har Rai was just 14 years old when he became a guru. He retained the fairly large number of troops that his grandfather had assembled. But he also cultivated peaceful relations with the ruling Mughal leader, Dara Shikoh. These efforts led to a time of peaceful coexistence. However, Dara Shikoh lost the Mughal throne to his brother Aurangzeb in 1658.

The new emperor summoned Guru Har Rai to explain his relationship with his deposed brother. Instead of going himself, Har Rai sent his oldest son, Ram Rai, in his place. Ram Rai tried to keep the peace and appease the new Mughal leader. He was asked to explain a line in the Sikh scripture that seemed to belittle Muslims. Ram Rai suggested that the line might have been inaccurately transcribed.

Guru Har Rai Ji

But questioning the holy scripture was not acceptable. So upon hearing what his son had done, Har Rai banished his son. Just before his death in 1661, Guru Har Rai named his younger son, five-year-old Har Krishan, the next guru. At the time of his death, Har Rai had been the Sikh guru for 17 years.

The Shortest-Serving Guru: Guru Har Krishan

Har Krishan's reign as the eighth Sikh guru lasted only three years. His older brother, Ram Rai, was still a friend of the Mughal leader Aurangzeb and lived at Aurangzeb's palace in Delhi. Ram Rai complained about his younger brother being named guru. So Guru

Guru Har Rai was a firm believer that hymns were good for the heart and soul.

Har Krishan too was summoned to Aurangzeb's palace to prove his leadership.

While Guru Har Krishan was in Delhi, he met with the many Sikhs who lived there. He ministered to both Sikhs and Hindus who were victims of severe cholera and smallpox epidemics that raged through the city. Because of this close contact, he contracted the dangerous disease smallpox. He died in 1664 at eight years old. Before he passed away, his granduncle, Tegh Bahadur, became the next guru.

Another Martyr: Guru Tegh Bahadur

Guru Tegh Bahadur became the ninth Sikh guru in 1664. Sikh historians said Guru Tegh Bahadur was more like a beloved grandfather than a granduncle to Guru Har Krishan.

HOW TEGH BAHADUR BECAME GURU

According to Sikh tradition, Tegh Bahadur became guru in an interesting way. Makhan Shah, a seafaring trader, was caught in a terrible storm while at sea. He vowed to give the Sikh guru 501 gold mohurs, or coins, if he were allowed to live. The storm calmed and he lived. Shah traveled to the city of Bakala in Punjab to find the guru. Meanwhile, many people heard of the death of the Guru Har Krishan and rushed to Bakala to claim the title of guru. Shah, finding all the guru hopefuls, decided to test them. He put before each candidate two gold mohurs. Then he came to Tegh Bahadur. Bahadur asked the trader for the other 499 gold mohurs he had promised during the storm. Makhan Shah rushed to the rooftop and exclaimed that he had found the true guru. Only the true, all-knowing guru could know about the vow Makhan had made while at sea.

Guru Tegh Bahadur traveled to many regions in India to spread the word of Sikhism. One of the things he is best known for is the addition of his hymns to the Sikh holy scriptures. These hymns were the last addition to the scriptures. The second thing Guru Tegh Bahadur is known for is his martyrdom. Under the reign of Guru Tegh Bahadur, the Sikhs decided to try their luck and move back to the plains of Punjab. This did not end well for Guru Tegh Bahadur, however. Sikh records say he was arrested by Mughal authorities for helping Hindu priests of Kashmir resist Mughal attempts to convert them to Islam. Guru Tegh Bahadur was then offered the choice between converting to Islam or death. He chose death and was immediately beheaded in 1675. Sikh Guru Tegh Bahadur gave up his life for the freedom of religion.

Tegh Bahadur was remembered as an adamant defender of religious freedom.

THE LAST HUMAN GURU

With the death of his father, Tegh Bahadur, Gobind Rai became the tenth guru of the Sikhs in 1675 when he was nine years old. His name was later changed to Gobind Singh. Guru Gobind Singh is considered the second-most important of the gurus after Guru Nanak.

When he was five years old, Gobind Rai was taken to Anandpur in northern India to study poetry, warfare, and the Sanskrit and Persian languages. After becoming the guru, he continued his education in the Himalayan foothills of northern India. There he grew to manhood as the ruler of a small state, battling other leaders in the area.

Guru Gobind Singh grew quickly as a military leader. Although he fought many battles, he also helped establish peace with the Mughals for a short time with Emperor Bahadur Shah in 1707. But the peace did not last long.

Guru Gobind Singh, *right*, meeting Bahadur Shah, a Mughal emperor, in 1707

A painting depicts Guru Gobind Singh and the original five panj pyare.

The Initiation of the Khalsa

Long before peace with the Mughals, Guru Gobind Singh established a new order of Sikh called the Khalsa, which means "pure." All those who went through the initiation into this new order swore their allegiance to only the guru. In the beginning of this order, around 1699, the Khalsa was open to volunteers. Later, it became the initiation, or baptism, into Sikhism for everyone.

According to legend, at the Baisakhi festival in 1699, Guru Gobind Singh gathered thousands of Sikhs together. When the crowd quieted, he asked if there was any Sikh who would volunteer to show his loyalty and devotion to the guru by giving up his head. The crowd was astounded and very quiet. The guru repeated his demand. Eventually, one man came forward. The guru took the man into the tent and came back out with a bloody sword. He then asked for another volunteer. In all, four more men volunteered to lose their heads. Each volunteer in his turn was taken into the tent, and each time the guru returned with a bloody sword.

By the time the guru had taken the fifth volunteer into the tent, the crowd was beginning to think he had gone crazy. But then the five Sikhs were led, alive, back outside. The guru administered the sword baptism to the five Sikhs. This would become the initiation ceremony for admittance to the Khalsa community. Those warriors would assist the guru in protecting Sikh land and authority against other local rulers and the Mughal Empire. The creation of the Khalsa warriors would bring about enormous political and cultural changes in Punjab over the next several decades. The first five men were the original panj pyare of the Sikhs. These men, and others like them, would carry on the initiation ceremony for the Khalsa from that day forward. Today, five panj pyare are seen at the front of every Sikh parade celebrating holy days and festivals. Any five Khalsa Sikhs can serve as a panj pyare. However, they must live their lives according to the Sikh Rehat Maryada.

Guru Gobind Singh declared before his death that his successor for all time would be the book of scriptures that guided Sikhs' spiritual life. Thus, Guru Granth Sahib now had the same status as a living guru.

Fighting Sikhs

Over the next few years after establishing the Khalsa, Guru Gobind Singh fought several battles, winning some and losing others. He was eventually assassinated in 1708. This last human guru continues to be the ideal toward which Sikhs strive.

Before his death, the guru had authorized his follower Banda Singh Bahadur to punish any persecutors of the Sikhs. By rallying peasants throughout Punjab, Banda and the Khalsa warriors gained control of the province from the mighty Mughal Empire that ruled much of South Asia. Even after Banda was captured, tortured, and killed, the Sikhs continued to fight. Many *misls*, or small bands of fighting men, formed to combat Afghan invaders who wanted to conquer India. The Afghan ruler attacked nine times between 1747 and 1769. The 65 misls protecting Punjab combined into 12 main

RULES FOR THE KHALSA WARRIORS

When Guru Gobind Singh created the Khalsa, he introduced an expanded code of conduct for those initiated. There are five outward signs, called the five Ks, that each warrior is expected to have. They are *kesh*, uncut hair; *kangha*, a wooden comb; *kachera*, cotton shorts; *kirpan*, a sword; and *kara*, a steel or iron bracelet.

The kesh signifies the sanctity of the body as a holy temple. It represents disciplined holiness. The kangha also represents holiness and signifies the importance of keeping the hair clean. The kangha is worn in the hair, which is tied in a knot. The men started a custom of covering their hair in a turban. This was to keep the hair and comb in place. The last three Ks relate to being warriors. The kachera, which look similar to loose-fitting white boxer shorts, are a sign of self-control. Some scholars thought the longer-than-usual shorts were more adapted to fighting than other forms of clothing. The kirpan stands for defending the community, seeking justice, and defending the weak. The kara protects the wrist during battle. Its circular shape is also thought to be a reminder of God, and some Sikhs described it as a "handcuff" to God. To others, the kara is a reminder to use their hands only for good purposes.

groups and defeated the Afghans. Eventually, all the misls united under one Sikh leader, Maharaja Ranjit Singh.

Under Maharaja Ranjit Singh's leadership, the Sikhs enjoyed 40 years as an independent country from 1799 to 1839. Singh is still considered an ideal leader by the Sikhs. He is remembered with pride and honored to this day.

British Rule

When Ranjit Singh died in 1839, the Sikhs started fighting among themselves. This fighting went on for ten years. The country was in disarray. In 1849, the British took advantage of this and expanded their control in India to include the Sikh country in their colonial empire. Even though the Sikhs resented the British for conquering their country, they were recruited into the British army because of their fierceness and fighting ability. The British liked the Sikh warriors so much that they allowed them to continue their Khalsa traditions in their British army units. These Sikh soldiers traveled to other countries in Southeast Asia and brought back stories that led to Sikh migration to those countries.

The Sikhs' resentment of their British rulers continued through the first half of the 1900s. Despite these lingering feelings, many Sikh warriors again fought for the British during both World War I (1914–1918) and World War II

THE LION OF PUNJAB

Maharaja Ranjit Singh led the Sikhs in their glory days of being an independent country. He is called the Lion of Punjab and is still one of the Sikh faithful's most popular leaders. He put an end to invasions from beyond Punjab's western borders. His rule held together an empire of more than 100,000 square miles (260,000 sq km).[1] Maharaja Ranjit Singh's leadership style was very inclusive. Hindus, Muslims, and even Europeans played a part in his army and administration. Within a decade of his death, the state he created collapsed because of infighting among rival Sikh chiefs.

SIKH MARTIAL ART

The Sikh martial art, called *gatka*, is believed to have been developed by several of the gurus all the way back to Guru Nanak. It has been handed down through various teachers, called *ustads*. It is both a physical and spiritual practice.

Modern demonstrations of the art mostly combine sword and shield maneuvers to the sound of drums. But the original forms contained hand-to-hand combat, wrestling, and stick fighting as well. Serious practitioners master the art by combining meditation, prayer, and awareness with exercise, a healthy diet, and their fighting techniques.

During the British-Sikh wars, well-trained Sikh warriors killed many British soldiers. After the Sikh Empire ended, the British tried to exterminate the Sikh martial art and its teachers, but they did not succeed. Today, gatka is growing in popularity with young Sikhs, particularly in the United Kingdom and the United States.

(1939–1945). The Sikhs who had emigrated to other countries also fought for those nations, such as Canada and the United States, in both those wars.

A few years after World War II, in 1947, Sikh hopes of an independent country were dashed when India was granted its independence from the British. Their homeland in Punjab was divided between the new country of Pakistan and the country of India. Pakistan was made a Muslim nation, while India was to become a nondenominational country. But its government was largely influenced by Hinduism and Sikhism.

Fight for Sikhs' Land

Because of the historical negative feelings between the Sikhs and the Muslims, the Sikhs fled the much larger portion of Punjab for the relative security of the smaller Punjab area in India. The smaller Punjab

Jarnail Bhindranwale, *center*, was the Sikh extremist leader behind the attack on Amritsar in 1984.

area was further divided in 1966 based on the different languages spoken in the area, Hindu and Punjabi. The Punjabi speakers are mostly Sikhs. By the 1980s, the Sikhs won political control of Punjab, but militant Sikh factions wanted to secede from India and form an independent country of their own.

A major political battle took place in Punjab at the temple of Amritsar in 1984. Sikh separatists barricaded themselves in the temple. The Indian government sent in troops, and 450 to more than 1,000 people, including onlookers, were killed.[2] The Sikhs were chased from the temple. In retaliation, Sikh bodyguards to the Indian prime

SIKH SECTS

Not all Sikhs strictly followed the Sikh Rehat Maryada declared by Guru Gobind Singh. Two main groups, the Nirankaris and the Namdharis, believed that human gurus continued even after Gobind Singh's death. A third sect, the Akhand Kirtani Jatha, believe in a different interpretation of one of the five Ks. They think that the mandate to not cut one's hair really means the faithful should just wear a small turban under the main turban. In this sect, both men and women are required to wear this type of turban. The fourth major sect, the Sikh Dharma, also requires women to wear turbans. It was founded in the United States in 1971. It is commonly known as the 3HO: Healthy Happy Holy Organization. The 3HO emphasizes meditation and the practice of kundalini yoga, a tool in which a person's will controls the person's mental, physical and nervous energy. There are other groups of Sikhs who cut their hair and beards, do not carry all of the five Ks on their person, or do not strictly follow the Sikh code of conduct contained in the Sikh Rehat Maryada.

minister, Indira Gandhi, assassinated her. Although the Sikhs did not get the separate country they wanted, relative peace returned to Punjab by the 1990s. This movement toward peace was hastened in 2004 when Manmohan Singh, a Sikh, was named the prime minister of India.

The Sikhs' role as warriors is a long tradition that is tied to their religion. They proved themselves as fierce and loyal. Today, initiation into Khalsa Sikhism continues and is extended to both men and women.

WHERE IN THE WORLD ARE THE SIKHS?

With a few exceptions, the Sikhs stayed mostly in India until the late 1800s. After the British annexed the country in 1849, they encouraged Sikh farmers to move from the eastern part of Punjab to newly irrigated lands in the western part of that state, which is now in Pakistan.

Sikh warriors were highly recruited by the British because they were seen as possessing the warrior personality necessary for military service. Many of these Sikh servicemen were stationed around Southeast Asia, outside of India. Those deployments opened their eyes to new employment opportunities. After their service, they left India to settle in other Asian countries, such as modern-day Malaysia and Hong Kong. One hundred Sikh police officers went to

Maharaja Duleep Singh, former ruler of the Sikh Empire, submitted to British forces in 1846 during the first Anglo-Sikh War (1845–1846).

Sikh British soldiers in 1890

Hong Kong in 1867, and many Sikhs served in that capacity as police until well into the 1900s.

The 1800s

In the late 1800s, greater numbers of Sikhs started to move out of what was then India in search of jobs. The first Sikh to arrive in England was Maharaja Duleep Singh in 1849. He was the last ruler of the Sikh Empire in India. Duleep Singh had been overthrown by the British government and exiled to England. He was only 15 years old at the time.

Sikhs first went to East African countries in the 1890s to help build the Uganda railway. They were woodworkers, blacksmiths, and masons. These laborers typically returned to Punjab when their work ended. Other skilled Sikh laborers migrated to East Africa permanently. They eventually became part of the middle tier of the colonial society.

CANADA TURNS AWAY SHIPLOAD OF IMMIGRANTS

In 1908, Canada passed a regulation that required immigrants to have direct passage ticketing arrangements from their country of origin. The regulation primarily affected immigrants from India and Japan since those countries did not have direct passage to Canada. There were court challenges to discriminatory Canadian immigration laws of the early 1900s. Those challenges were not effective in changing the laws. So in 1914, the ship *Komagata Maru* arrived in Canada from Hong Kong with 376 South Asian immigrants to challenge the immigration laws. The hope was that since they were already there, they would be allowed to stay. Authorities in Canada's harbor in Vancouver held the ship for two months. It was forced to return to Asia with all its passengers. The discriminatory laws held fast.

Many worked in professional positions in fields such as administration, education, and employment and social services.

The first flow of Sikh immigration into Canada began in the late 1890s after a Sikh major in the British army passed through the country. His stories of the jobs available encouraged his countrymen to move to Canada. At about the same time, the first four Sikhs to come to the United States entered California in 1899.

North America in the 1900s

The first big wave of Sikhs arrived in Vancouver, British Columbia, in 1903. These men were attracted by high wages in Canada and temporarily left their families for employment. After the first Sikhs moved to the United States, many more followed, and by 1915, approximately 6,000 Sikhs had arrived on the West Coast of the United States.[1] Because of their farming backgrounds in India, most

The treatment of Sikhs has come a long way in Canada since they first arrived in the country in 1903. In 2015, Prime Minister Justin Trudeau, *center*, helped make amends by visiting a gurdwara in Ottawa.

Sikhs settled in California's Central Valley agricultural region. Others worked in Oregon sawmills and on railroad construction.

Similar to the Chinese and Japanese immigrants to Canada and the United States before them, the Sikhs faced prejudice and discrimination. In 1907, the Canadian government effectively cut off all legal immigration of the Sikhs. Despite this, undocumented illegal immigration continued on routes

SIKHS IN THE UNITED STATES

When the United States further eased immigration laws in the 1960s, Sikhs from India applied to US universities. Most of those students chose to stay in the United States after graduation. These highly educated and professional graduates added a new element to Sikhism in the country. No longer were Sikhs a mostly rural occurrence in the country.

Narinder Singh Kapany and his spouse, Satinder, used the easier immigration laws enacted after World War II to their advantage. He earned a doctoral degree in physics from the University of London. He and his wife arrived in the United States in 1955. After teaching at several universities, he eventually settled in the area now known as Silicon Valley in California. There he started a fiber optics and optoelectronics business that earned him millions of dollars. Satinder started her own successful real estate investment firm.

The Kapanys used their wealth to support the Sikh community in the United States. They established the Sikh Foundation, an organization that sought to start Sikhism studies at California universities. In 1997, they paid for a university faculty position, called an endowment, at the University of California in Santa Barbara.

through Washington State in the United States into Canada. In 1913, California passed laws prohibiting Asians from owning land. Other western states soon did the same. In 1917, the United States banned immigration from South Asia. These laws also prevented Sikhs already in the United States from becoming citizens. Further, they could not send for their families to join them. Until the Great

Depression of the 1930s, when jobs became scarce, Sikhs still came into the United States illegally across its border with Mexico.

Discriminatory immigration legislation against South Asians, including the Sikhs, was gradually removed in Canada starting in 1951. By the 1960s, the United States opened immigration from India. Canadian nondiscriminatory legislation in 1967 led to further increases in the Canadian Sikh population. The Canadian government legalized the status of illegal immigrants and apologized for some of the prejudiced treatment of the Sikhs.

The United Kingdom in the 1900s

The first wave of Sikh immigration to the United Kingdom began at the end of World War I and lasted until 1950. Most of those immigrants came after 1947, when India gained its independence from the United Kingdom. Most of the Sikhs stayed in India, but a large number of what were considered lower-caste Sikhs immigrated to England for unskilled job opportunities. Many Sikh men in this wave started out as door-to-door

IMMIGRATION TO MAINLAND EUROPE

Sikhs began moving to mainland Europe in the 1970s. Sikhs first went to Germany, Belgium, and France because of comparatively restrictive UK immigration policies. Jobs in the dairy industry brought a large number of Sikhs to Italy. The first Sikhs to arrive in a Nordic country landed in Norway in 1969. As of 2017, Norway had the highest number of Sikhs among the Nordic countries, with 14,000.[2]

PERSPECTIVES

KHUSHWANT SINGH: SIKH AUTHOR

Khushwant Singh was one of the best-known authors and journalists in India. He lived from 1915 to 2014. He wrote more than 80 books and served as editor for several newspapers. He joined the Indian Foreign Service and spent time in Ottawa, Canada; London, England; and Paris, France. Eventually, he returned to India to write. His writings were known to be very blunt and truthful about the violence and corruption in India. Although he loved India, he was one of its most persistent critics.

Singh's best-known novel, *Train to Pakistan*, told of the religious violence done by Hindus, Muslims, and Sikhs to each other as India was being divided in 1947. As Muslims fled India to the new republic of Pakistan, they boasted of killing Hindus and Sikhs. The Sikhs and Hindus fleeing to India boasted of slaughtering Muslims. More than one million people died. "You kill my dog, I kill your cat" was how he described the revenge killings. "It's a childish and bloody game, and it can't go on."[3]

salesmen and eventually became shopkeepers and rental agents. Their descendants moved into many other professions.

In the late 1950s and early 1960s, the second wave of Sikhs entered England. Many had been farmers in the Punjab state. But the amount of land they planted dwindled as each generation split the land further among their sons. At this time, British immigration policy and plentiful job opportunities were very favorable to the Sikhs. Many of these Sikh men, despite their religious teachings, cut their hair and removed their turbans to get jobs. After these men got settled, their wives joined them in England. Unlike past Sikh immigrant women, these women found jobs too.

In the 1970s, East African nations gained their independence from British rule. This was

A group of Sikhs standing outside their gurdwara in Toronto, Canada, in the 1970s

almost 100 years after the Sikhs first immigrated to East African nations. East African leaders wanted more of their own people to be leaders and craftsmen. They fired many non-Africans from their jobs, and many were expelled. A number of them moved to England. The Sikhs left East Africa and joined family members who had immigrated to England directly from Punjab. This third wave of Sikhs chose not to give up their cultural identity and kept their turbans and other Sikh traditions.

HOW SIKHS PRACTICE THEIR RELIGION

Sikhism as practiced by devout Sikhs is a daily activity. The importance to the Sikhs of their holy scripture, Guru Granth Sahib, is proved by its usage throughout the day. Sikhs begin their day by bathing between three and six o'clock in the morning and reciting a specific hymn called *Japji Sahib*. Other passages from the holy book are read in the morning too. Every morning, a passage from Sikh scripture is broadcast across the world via the internet from the Golden Temple in Amritsar. This passage is the instruction from Guru Granth Sahib for all Sikhs to follow for that day.

At 5:30 in the morning, in gurdwaras around the world, an attendant to the Guru Granth Sahib opens the sacred scripture. From a page chosen at random, the attendant sings the hymn at the top

Sikhs observe many holidays, including Shaheedi Jor Mela, which is a three-day festival that pays tribute to the two martyred sons of Guru Gobind Singh.

Sikhs are required to recite five prayers every day.

of the left-hand page. This is the local daily guidance for the Sikhs of that temple. This guidance is displayed in the temple foyer for all to see.

In the early evening, several compositions of the gurus are recited. The morning and evening readings end with works by Guru Gobind Singh. At the end of the day, several hymns by Gurus Nanak, Ram Das, and Arjan are sung or chanted. The purpose of reading and singing frequently is to keep *nam*, or divine reality, uppermost in one's mind during the day.

Life-Cycle Rites

Reformers of Sikhism in the early 1900s wanted to get rid of any connection to Hinduism. A way to do this was to start their own rites for naming children and holding funerals. They abandoned the Hindu way of choosing a child's name, which uses an initial from an astrological reading. Sikh parents now take their babies to a gurdwara, where the granthi, or temple steward, opens the sacred scriptures to a random page. The initial of the first word at the top of the left-hand page becomes the child's name initial. The family then decides the child's name. Then, the granthi announces this name, which is followed by Kaur, for a girl, or Singh, for a boy.

The funeral rite for Sikhs also changed. Instead of following the Hindu funeral traditions, Sikhs turn to their sacred scriptures for comfort and guidance. The body is placed on a funeral pyre, and the granthi recites a prayer. The eldest son of the deceased then lights the funeral pyre, and a prayer is recited as the body burns. If there is no eldest son, another male close to the family may be selected to start the fire. In the days after the cremation is completed, the entire holy scripture is read. This is usually done in a continuous 48-hour reading or over a seven- to ten-day period. The ashes of the loved one are then taken to a sacred site for scattering.

An initiation rite, similar to baptism in Christianity, is conducted to bring a person into the Sikh Khalsa community. The rite was first conducted according to the Sikh code of conduct issued by the tenth guru, Gobind Singh. That code, called the Sikh Rehat Maryada, was modernized in 1931. Now, six Sikhs who have already been initiated carry out the ritual. Sweetened water is poured into a large iron bowl and stirred by a double-edged sword. The water is called amrit, or nectar. After some prayers,

HOW ARE SIKHS NAMED?

Sikhs usually have three names. The first name typically includes sounds that are associated with God. Some names begin or end with *preet*, which means "love." Others include *deep*, meaning "light," or *jit*, meaning "victory." For example, *Amandeep* means "light of peace," combining *aman*, or peace, with *deep*, which is light.

The traditional middle names of Sikhs date back to 1699. Girls are named *Kaur*, which means "princess" or "daughter of a king." Boys are given the middle name of *Singh*, which means "lion." These two names promote equality.

Sikhs in Birmingham, England, drink the amrit holy nectar during the Khalsa initiation ceremony.

each candidate drinks five handfuls of the amrit. Each time, the Sikh offering the amrit exclaims, "Praise to the Guru's Khalsa! Praise to the Guru's victory!" Some amrit is then sprinkled five times on the initiate's hair and eyes. Then everyone repeats a portion of prayers and listens to some of the code of conduct requirements.

PERSPECTIVES

WOMEN'S ROLE IN FUNERAL RITES

Nikky-Guninder Kaur Singh was born in India and is now a professor of religion at Colby College in Maine. Singh's mother passed away in the 1990s. She traveled to India for the funeral.

Singh described the beautiful and loving preparations of her mother's body for cremation in the *Journal of Feminist Studies in Religion*. The long-standing tradition in Sikhism is for the oldest son to light the funeral pyre. Her only brother was not able to attend the funeral. She said, "I did not even question" the choice of a male family friend to light the fire. "I was not even aware of being eliminated."[1]

By past traditions, only men could gather the personal articles, ashes, and bones of her mother. Her mother's bones were cleansed and placed in a bag for their last journey. No women were allowed to touch these either, but Singh asked to hold the bones as a last goodbye. She was reluctantly allowed to do so.

Singh began wondering how the first Sikh guru's teaching of gender equality had changed so much over time. "What was the feminist vision of Guru Nanak? How did he begin feminizing rituals?"[2] Singh continues to work toward the refeminization of Sikhism.

The requirements for those initiated into the Sikh Khalsa include wearing the five Ks. They must also avoid four sins: cutting one's hair, eating meat prepared in Islamic fashion, committing adultery, and using tobacco. Any Khalsa Sikh who commits these sins must confess in public and be reinitiated.

Code of Conduct: Sikh Rehat Maryada

The code of conduct issued in the 1700s by Guru Gobind Singh was not consistent with and even contradicted some of the principles taught by the other nine gurus. Therefore, many Sikhs did not strictly follow Gobind Singh's code. Finally, in 1931, the Sikhs settled upon a set of consistent guidelines covering religious and social procedures for Sikhs worldwide.

These guidelines are called the Sikh Rehat Maryada.

This revised code of conduct addresses everything from what a Sikh is, to individual Sikhs' private lives, to how the sacred scriptures should be read and sung, to living according to the gurus' teachings. It also is specific as to how the Karah Prasad, which is served in various Sikh ceremonies and services, is to be made.

Holy Days and Festivals throughout the Year

In addition to the Baisakhi celebration in mid-April, Sikhs observe seven other major occurrences of importance during the year. The birthdays of the

Meat is not served during langar because Sikhs want the meal to be available to all, including people who follow different religious rules about meat eating.

first and tenth gurus, Guru Nanak and Guru Gobind Singh, are celebrated. There are also days devoted to the martyrdom of Guru Arjan and Guru Tegh Bahadur.

One of the three other major festivals celebrates the beginning of the Guru Granth Sahib as a living being. The celebration is called a *gurpurb*, a holy day of the gurus. Bandi Chhor Divas, celebrated in October, celebrates the release of the sixth guru, Hargobind, from the Mughals. The final festival, Hola Mohalla, originated as an alternative to a Hindu holiday. The first gatherings featured martial arts displays and mock battles. Now it is celebrated with military parades.

Keeping God uppermost in one's thoughts is the ideal for the Sikhs. All the activities of the day, the rites of passage, and the celebrations encourage that ideal. Both the personal and professional lives of Sikhs aim to put the beliefs and ideals of Sikhism into action.

COMMON MISCONCEPTIONS ABOUT SIKHS

In January 2015, a study conducted in the United States by the National Sikh Campaign found that 60 percent of the Americans participating in the study admitted knowing very little about Sikhs.[1] Rajwant Singh, a cofounder of the campaign, said that the Sikhs are not well known and are often misunderstood. This is despite the fact that they first immigrated to the United States more than 100 years ago and are an integral part of American life. The study found that many Americans assume that anyone who wears a turban is Muslim, which the Sikhs are not. This false assumption led to persecution and hate crimes against Sikhs after the September 11 terror attacks in 2001.

Another cofounder of the National Sikh Campaign, Gurwin Singh Ahuja, thought the mistaken perception of Sikhs was sad because

Hindus, such as this man, follow a religion that is very different from Sikhism. It's important to ask people about their religion before assuming that they practice one or another.

they have very modern values. Specifically, he mentioned the Sikh beliefs that "men and women are equal and that all faiths have the right to practice."[2] An encouraging sign is that the US millennial generation and those ages 16 to 34 are more likely to see the Sikhs in a positive light than the older generations.[3]

Sikhism Misconceptions

Generalizations about who and what Sikhs are can be a result of not having good information about Sikhism. Those errors in thinking can lead to unkind and hurtful actions toward Sikhs or any other group of people.

One such misconception is that the Sikh religion is an offshoot of Hinduism or Islam. Sikhism did spring up in the middle of Hindu culture and under strong control by the Mughals, who were Muslims. However, Sikhs believe their new faith, called Sikhism, was revealed to the first guru, Nanak, by God.

Another misconception is that all Sikhs are Indian. It is true that the vast majority of Sikhs are born and live in India, but

Sikhism is a religion and not a nationality. Sikhs born in Canada are Canadians, just as those born in France are French.

It is also important to note that no one is forced to become a Sikh, and anyone can become a Sikh if he or she so desires. Gurdwaras welcome all people regardless of their religious, cultural, or racial background. Neither does Sikhism prohibit its members from visiting churches outside the religion. They are free to visit mosques, churches, or synagogues.

The idea that anyone with a beard and wearing a turban is from the Middle East and is a Muslim or terrorist is another misconception affecting the Sikhs. As part of their religion, Sikhs must keep their heads covered at all times. The turban is a symbol of Sikh faith. However, turbans are also worn as part of the cultural dress of many countries by people who are not Sikh.

SIKHISM AS A UNIQUE RELIGION

Early Western scholars mistakenly thought Sikhism came out of Hinduism. However, the Sikhs say it did not. Sikhism has all the qualities of a separate and unique religion. It has its own scripture that is separate and different from those of other religions. Sikhism has its own ceremonies for birth, marriage, and death. It also has its own places of worship that are, again, separate from those of other religions.

Ignorance Leads to Hate Crimes

In the years following the September 11 terror attacks, Sikhs were subject to many hate crimes.

THE SIKH TURBAN

Sikh turbans are usually 13 to 22 feet (4 to 7 m) of finely made cotton that is tightly wound around the head. Although the turban is not generally required to be worn by Sikh codes of conduct, Khalsa Sikh men consider it an essential sign of their commitment. Any disrespect to the turban is considered disrespect for all Sikhs.

Turbans come in many colors that mostly reflect the preference of the wearer. However, the saffron-colored turban came to symbolize Sikhs who sought an independent Sikh state in India. Also, a man is more likely to wear a red, orange, or pink turban for his own marriage ceremony or that of one of his children.

The word *turban* is thought to have originated in what is now Iran. In Iran, leaders wear a white or black turban. Desert peoples in Africa have historically used turbans to keep sand from their faces.

Because the terrorists who committed the attacks were Muslim extremists, Sikhs were automatically believed to belong to this group solely based on their outward appearance. Some people discriminated against Sikhs because they incorrectly believed everyone who was Muslim (or in this case, looked Muslim) was a terrorist. More than 700 incidents of bias or violence against Sikhs were reported between 2001 and 2012, according to the Sikh Coalition.[4] In 2012, six Sikhs were killed by a shooter at one of their temples in Wisconsin. The 2012 shootings sparked an advertising campaign by

the Sikhs to inform other US citizens about who they are and
what they believe.

Racism against the Sikhs still festers in Canada too. In
September 2017, at a political campaign rally for the leadership
of the New Democratic Party in Ontario, Canada, candidate
Jagmeet Singh was verbally attacked. Singh, a Sikh, was
accused of supporting Muslim sharia law and the Muslim
Brotherhood. However, he went on to win the leadership race.
Singh was seen as being on his way to possibly becoming
the first Sikh prime minister of Canada in 2019. Erin Tolley, a
university associate professor in Canada, said that although
Canada promotes multiculturalism, racist sentiment is alive
and growing more vocal. She thinks these racist attitudes
can discourage all types of minorities from running for
political office.

Attacks on Children

The biggest concern for many Sikhs in the United States is the
upsurge of bullying against Sikh children in schools. According

After the 2012 terrorist attack on a Wisconsin Sikh temple, some Sikhs, including Harpreet Singh Saini, testified before a US Senate judiciary committee on "Hate Crimes and the Threat of Domestic Extremism."

to Simran Jeet Singh, a professor of religion at Trinity University, "Statistics show that in some US communities, Sikh children are bullied at more than three times the national average."[5]

Singh went on to say that recent politicians who fan religious and cultural hatred to win votes have incited increased violence against different cultures and religions. Prejudice and discrimination are becoming more open and violent. It is not just the Sikhs who are targeted, but this community in particular has been greatly affected by the growing prejudice.

SIKH STUDENTS TEACH TEACHERS

For four years, students in North Potomac, Maryland, taught a free class about Sikhism to their teachers. In 2016, the state approved the class to count for official teacher training. The training of teachers about the Sikh faith will give them the knowledge they need to head off religion-based bullying in their classrooms and schools. The students hope to take the class nationwide and are training other students in Fresno, California, and Phoenix, Arizona, on how to start the same program.

BEING SIKH IN THE MODERN WORLD

In the late 1900s, Sikh historian and journalist Khushwant Singh was fearful of Sikhism being absorbed into Hinduism. He thought this was the result of Sikhs abandoning the Khalsa identity. But in India it appeared that religious apathy and uncontrolled shopping by young Punjabi men were the real reasons. Those men were developing a more contemporary look and adopting the consumerism that was prevalent in Europe and North America in the previous 50 years. On the other hand, young Sikhs outside of India were showing an eagerness to identify as Sikh as well as citizens of Canada, the United Kingdom, Malaysia, or whatever country they lived in. Some of those outside of India were also showing greater commitment to the Khalsa Sikh ideal.

Sikhs have been able to take their ancient traditions and adapt them to the modern world.

Raising Sikh Children in the Modern World

Like many parents who immigrate to a new country, the Sikhs were concerned that their children were losing the knowledge of and commitment to their religious faith. A *New York Times* article in 1998 recounted Sikh parents' worries. They described their children's ability to chant rap songs but not their holy scriptures. The children were able to recite the Ten Commandments of the Christian faith but not the names of the ten Sikh gurus.

Sikh families throughout the world face the same challenge: how to raise their children as Sikhs following the

Whenever a Sikh child is born, the entire community celebrates.

divine will or commands of Guru Nanak in a world that is changing. In Guru Nanak's time, children followed in their parents' footsteps. Their work, marriages, and life decisions flowed from the family. That is no longer the case for Sikhs worldwide. Sikh parents can no longer expect their children to do things the way they did. In an article about a Sikh school in Amritsar, Saraswati Kaur Khalsa said they need to find ways to "kindle a love for the Guru in their hearts, to love their turban, and to learn how the teachings of the Guru are relevant in the world."[1]

Gender Equality?

At the time of the first ten gurus, women were very low in society. Both the Hindus and Muslims considered them men's property and inferior to men. When Guru Nanak first founded Sikhism, he stated that women and men were equal. This was a shocking statement for that time period.

When looking at gender equality from the view of modern Western cultures, things do

SIKH WORLDWIDE INTERNET COMMUNITY

More and more Sikhs are turning to the internet and social media to gain knowledge of their religion and discuss it with others. As of 2014, there were approximately 2,000 Sikh websites and 500 Sikh discussion groups. As many as 500 Sikh Facebook groups exist.[2] An increasing number of Sikhs use Twitter. YouTube videos of Sikh celebrations worldwide make Sikhism more accessible. The internet makes the sacred scriptures more available to average Sikhs, and they can make virtual visits to sacred sites not in their own countries.

SIKH WOMEN LESS EQUAL?

Is there less gender equality in Sikhism than in other religions or countries? Not according to the 2016 Global Gender Gap Report from the World Economic Forum. Gender equality does not exist anywhere on Earth, according to the report.

The report looked at gender-based differences in access to health resources, education, earning power, and political representation across the globe. The report recognized that a country's culture is one of the main contributors to the gaps between women and men in the areas measured. So, Sikh women may have more equality in countries that, in general, have cultures in which gender equality is more highly valued.

Of the 144 countries included in the report, the United Kingdom ranked number 20 in gender equality. Canada came in at number 35, and the United States ranked 45th. India came in at number 87 in terms of overall gender equality. The top 4 ranked countries were all Scandinavian.[3]

not appear so equal. The differences between the ideal and what happens in daily life become quite obvious.

Sikh writer Upinder Jit Kaur attempted to explain the contrast between the ideal and the reality of women's equality in Punjab as the result of living within the larger Hindu society. The Hindu societal norms saw women as lesser people, according to Kaur. In other words, the inequality of Sikh women was caused by something outside Sikhism.

Some Sikhs do not deny the difference but say that the position of women in Sikhism is superior to the position of Islamic and Christian women in their religions. These Sikhs suggest that Sikh women have access to religious positions that Islamic and Christian women cannot attain. In theory, Sikh women have the right to become granthis in Sikh gurdwaras, musicians, and members of the panj pyare. However, they very seldom become granthis or panj pyare. During the langar, the women are urged to cook, wash dishes, and clean, but they are not allowed to enter the special room in the temple where the Sikh holy scriptures are placed.

Many Sikh women serve as activists, especially when attacks have taken place against Sikhs.

A Sikh woman in the United States, Valarie Kaur, says that women such as herself may be part of the problem. Although they may talk a lot about women's equality, they are soaked in a culture that is historically male centered. The great Sikh women thinkers, warriors, and poets are considered only in relation to the men they supported. The result is that Sikh girls of today are told they are equal, but they are expected to fill traditional female roles.

Overcoming Gender Bias

Despite the observed gender inequality in Sikhism, there are Sikh women throughout history that girls can look to as role models. For example, Rani Sada Kaur became the first female Sikh military commander. Taking over for her husband, who died in battle against other Sikh chieftains, she took the warrior role, and she led battles that secured the first Sikh Empire. She was a close adviser to Maharaja Ranjit Singh of that empire.

Amrita Pritam is considered the leading poet of the Punjabi language in the 1900s. Born in 1919, she represented the growing importance of Sikh women writers, poets, and scholars. She was known for the beautiful way she described the people of India and for her description of the harrowing tragedy they at times endured. Her most famous works are "Ode to Waris Shah" and *Pinjar*, a novel, which was later translated as *The Skeleton*.

Amrit Singh is a powerful civil rights lawyer in the United States. She fought the US government in cases related to torture, indefinite detention, and discrimination after the September 2001

Amrita Pritam died in 2005.

Manmohan Singh served as prime minister of India from 2004 to 2014.

terror attacks. She symbolizes the current generation of Sikh women lawyers doing battle in the courtroom.

Dr. Anarkali Kaur Honaryar became the first elected non-Muslim in the government of Afghanistan in 2010. She is a tireless protector of minority and women's rights in that country. She is another modern model of brave and influential Sikh women.

Notable Sikhs Worldwide

Manmohan Singh was the first Sikh to become prime minister of India. Before he became prime minister, he was India's influential finance minister. With a doctoral degree from Oxford University in England, he was the most educated Indian prime minister in history.

Canadian Sikhs made headway in becoming valued members in their adopted country. In 2000,

AN INTERNATIONAL BOARDING SCHOOL FOR SIKHISM

A boarding school in Amritsar helps students from around the world become well educated in Sikhism. The Miri Piri Academy (MPA) offers all the regular high school subjects, including music, drama, and sports activities. Although the school teaches Sikhism, students from other faiths enroll too.

One student, Gagandeep Singh, put it this way: "Before I was a Sikh by birth, but now I am actually living as a Sikh. I wish to live as a Sikh my whole life and follow the Sikh spiritual path forever."[4] After his graduation from MPA, he enrolled at Humber College in Toronto, Canada, to pursue studies in health and fitness science.

Sikhism will continue to grow and focus on equality, even as the world continues to change.

Ujjal Singh Dosanjh was elected premier of British Columbia. In that same province, a Sikh, Lieutenant-Colonel Harjit Sajjan, was made the commander of an army regiment in 2011. This was the same regiment that had turned away a shipload of Sikh immigrants on the *Komagata Maru* almost 100 years earlier. Sajjan later became the minister of national defence in 2015.

Philanthropic Activities

Helping the poor, the oppressed, and those in need is one of the basic rules of Sikhism. One of the ways Sikhs fulfill this philanthropic belief is through their charitable organizations. For example, the Sikh Foundation International is based in Palo Alto, California. Although its main purpose is to spread education and awareness of Sikhism, it is involved in other charitable activities. The foundation was involved in relief efforts in Texas after the devastating Hurricane Harvey in September 2017.

PERSPECTIVES

AN AMERICAN TEENAGER'S PERSPECTIVE

An American teenager (name unknown) put into words her concerns about growing up Sikh in the United States in an article from 1994 called "Things That Make You Ask 'Kion?' [Why?]." In it, she said, "We find that [our parents] just don't understand us and vice versa and along with this lack of understanding comes the inability to communicate."[5] She said it was more than just the generational gap but also the cultural gap. She objected to traditional Sikh values, which "still include double standards in the upbringing of Sikh boys and girls." She went on to say that "Sikh teenagers today are confused and need answers, not lectures or condemnation. They want answers dealing with questions on hair, the opposite sex, peer pressure, and the double standards society holds for girls." In concluding her statements, she said, "Above all I am asking that all Sikh parents should deal with their American Sikh teenagers with an understanding that certain dimensions of their familial lives have changed with the change of country and culture."[6]

Another organization, Khalsa Aid, is located outside London in the United Kingdom. Besides ongoing aid to the Sikhs' historical homeland in Punjab, it has provided worldwide support for national emergencies. Khalsa Aid provided support for the refugee crisis in Greece in 2016, the United Kingdom floods of 2015, and the Yemen Civil War of 2015. The victims of the Nepal earthquake, floods in Malawi, and Cyclone Marcia in Australia also benefited from Khalsa Aid in 2015.

In 1999, a group of Sikhs in New York City got together to support immigrant communities and formed a group called United Sikhs. Since then, they have grown into offices in other North American countries, Asia, and Europe. Now associated with the United Nations, the organization strives to protect and educate people affected by man-made and natural disasters. Further, it focuses on addressing violations of human and civil rights, regardless of who people are or where they come from.

From its earliest days, Sikhism has focused on equality, service to the community, and devotion to God. As years have passed, political and cultural concerns have changed how the Sikhs put those beliefs into practice. Practicing their beliefs in the modern world continues to be an ongoing undertaking for Sikhs.

ESSENTIAL FACTS

DATE FOUNDED

Sikhism was founded in 1499 by a man named Nanak in the Punjab region of India.

BASIC BELIEFS

During the first 200 years of Sikhism, ten holy men called gurus led the religion. The last human Sikh guru was Gobind Singh. In 1708, he decreed that henceforth a book of sacred scriptures would become the living guru for the rest of time.

Sikhs believe there is only one God. They also believe that all people, religions, ethnic groups, and genders are equal. Showing daily devotion to God is an important aspect of Sikhism, as is doing good works for others and defending those who cannot do it for themselves.

IMPORTANT HOLIDAYS AND EVENTS

- Baisakhi, a celebration of the initiation of the Khalsa
- Hola Mohalla, a martial arts festival that celebrates the military
- Bandi Chhor Divas, a celebration of the release of Guru Hargobind from the Muslim Mughals

Sikhs also have celebrations called gurpurbs, which mark special anniversaries, such as:

- The birthdate of Guru Nanak
- The birthdate of Guru Gobind Singh
- The martyrdom of Guru Arjan
- The martyrdom of Guru Tegh Bahadur
- The day Guru Granth Sahib became the living guru

FAITH LEADERS

- Guru Nanak, the founder of Sikhism
- Guru Angad
- Guru Amar Das
- Guru Ram Das
- Guru Arjan
- Guru Hargobind
- Guru Har Rai
- Guru Har Krishan
- Guru Tegh Bahadur
- Guru Gobind Singh, the last human guru
- Guru Granth Sahib, the holy book of Sikhism, considered the living guru

NUMBER OF PEOPLE WHO PRACTICE SIKHISM

There are approximately 25 million Sikhs worldwide.

QUOTE

"Before I was a Sikh by birth, but now I am actually living as a Sikh. I wish to live as a Sikh my whole life and follow the Sikh spiritual path forever."

—*Gagandeep Singh, a student at a Sikh boarding school in India*

GLOSSARY

ANNEX
To add to one's territory to make one's country larger.

APATHY
Lack of interest or enthusiasm.

APPEASE
To attempt to calm or win over.

ASTROLOGICAL
Having to do with astrology, the study of the movement of the stars and planets.

CASTE
A hereditary class in society.

CODE
A systematic collection of laws or regulations.

COMMEMORATE
To recall and show respect for something.

DEVOUT
Having or showing deep religious commitment.

ENLIGHTENMENT
The act of gaining spiritual knowledge or insight.

IMMIGRANT
A person who moves to a new country permanently.

MARTIAL ART
A form of self-defense or combat.

MEDITATE
To think deeply or focus one's mind for a period of time.

PHILANTHROPIC
Having to do with promoting the welfare of others, particularly through donating money.

PILGRIMAGE
A long journey to a sacred place to show devotion.

PYRE
A pile of burnable material, especially one for burning a body as part of a funeral ceremony.

SAFFRON
An orange-yellow color.

SALVATION
Deliverance from the power of sin.

SANCTITY
The state of being sacred or holy.

TRADITION
A custom or habit.

ADDITIONAL RESOURCES

SELECTED BIBLIOGRAPHY

Dhavan, Purnima. *When Sparrows Became Hawks: The Making of the Sikh Warrior Tradition, 1699–1799.* New York: Oxford UP, Inc. 2011. Print.

Mann, Gurinder Singh, et al. *Buddhists, Hindus, and Sikhs in America.* New York: Oxford UP. 2001. Print.

Singh, Nikky-Guninder Kaur. *Sikhism: An Introduction.* New York: I. B. Tauris, 2011. Print.

FURTHER READINGS

Nesbitt, Eleanor. *Sikhism: A Very Short Introduction.* 2nd ed. Oxford, UK: Oxford UP, 2016. Print.

Sheikh, Mohamed. *Emperor of the Five Rivers: The Life and Times of Maharaja Ranjit Singh.* London, UK: I. B. Tauris, 2017. Print.

ONLINE RESOURCES

Booklinks
NONFICTION NETWORK
FREE! ONLINE NONFICTION RESOURCES

To learn more about Sikhism, visit abdobooklinks.com. These links are routinely monitored and updated to provide the most current information available.

MORE INFORMATION

For more information on this subject, contact or visit the following organizations:

GOLDEN TEMPLE

Golden Temple Road
Amritsar, Punjab 143006, India
+91 183-255-3957
goldentempleamritsar.org

Visit the homeland of the Sikhs and the Golden Temple in Amritsar, India.

SIKH HERITAGE MUSEUM OF CANADA

125-2980 Drew Road
Mississauga, Ontario, Canada
416-587-5498
shmc.ca/contact-us

Canadians and visitors to Canada can visit the Sikh Heritage Museum of Canada. Exhibits have included Sikhs' roles during World War I and art inspired by meditation.

SOURCE NOTES

Chapter 1. Baisakhi Festival

1. Gurinder Singh Mann, Paul Numrich, and Raymond Williams. *Buddhists, Hindus, and Sikhs in America.* New York: Oxford UP, 2001. Print. 118.

2. Amber Pariona. "Countries with the Largest Sikh Populations." *Worldatlas.com.* World Atlas, 25 Apr. 2017. Web. 20 Aug. 2017.

3. Norman Buchignani. "South Asian Canadians." *The Canadian Encyclopedia.* The Government of Canada, 4 Mar. 2015. Web. 21 Aug. 2017.

4. "Baisakhi In Canada." *Baisakhifestival.com.* Society for the Confluence of Festivals in India, n.d. Web. 11 Sep. 2017.

5. Pariona, "Countries with the Largest Sikh Populations."

6. "About Sikhs." *Sikh Coalition.* Sikh Coalition, n.d. Web. 24 Jan. 2018.

7. Pariona, "Countries with the Largest Sikh Populations."

Chapter 2. What Is Sikhism?

1. "About Sikhs." *Sikh Coalition.* Sikh Coalition, n.d. Web. 24 Jan. 2018.

Chapter 3. The First Four Gurus of Sikhism

1. John M. Koller. *The Indian Way: An Introduction to the Philosophies and Religions of India*. 2nd ed. Abingdon, UK: Routledge Publishing, 2005. Print. 311.

2. "The Second Master Guru Angad (1504–1552)." *Sikhs.org*. Sikhs.org, 2011. Web. 16 Sep. 2017.

Chapter 4. The Militant Gurus

None.

Chapter 5. The Last Human Guru

1. Eleanor Nesbitt. *Sikhism: A Very Short Introduction*. 2nd ed. Oxford, UK: Oxford UP, 2016. Print. 64.

2. "Indian Army Storms Golden Temple." *History.com*. A&E Television Network, n.d. Web. 24 Jan. 2018.

Chapter 6. Where in the World Are the Sikhs?

1. Gurinder Singh Mann, Paul Numrich, and Raymond Williams. *Buddhists, Hindus, and Sikhs in America*. New York: Oxford UP, 2001. Print. 125.

2. Mann, Numrich, and Williams, *Buddhists, Hindus, and Sikhs,* 89–90.

3. Somini Sengupta. "Author Bears Steady Witness to Partition's Words." *New York Times*. New York Times, 21 Sept. 2006. Web. 24 Jan. 2018.

SOURCE NOTES CONTINUED

Chapter 7. How Sikhs Practice Their Religion

1. Doris R. Jakobsh. *Sikhism and Women: History, Texts, and Experience.* New Delhi, India: Oxford UP, 2010. Print. 207–208.

2. Jakobsh, *Sikhism and Women*, 228.

Chapter 8. Common Misconceptions about Sikhs

1. Robert MacPherson. "Americans Are Still Confusing Sikhs for Muslims." *BusinessInsider.com*. Business Insider, 28 Jan. 2015. Web. 1 Aug. 2017.

2. MacPherson, "Americans Are Still Confusing Sikhs."

3. MacPherson, "Americans Are Still Confusing Sikhs."

4. "Temple Shooting Dredges Up Memories of Long History of Bias Crimes against Sikhs." *Cnn.com*. Turner Broadcasting System, 6 Aug. 2012. Web. 2 Aug. 2017.

5. Murtaza Hussain. "Sikh Americans Fight for Civil Rights in Donald Trump's America." *The Intercept*. First Look Media, 14 Mar. 2016. Web. 16 Sep. 2017.

Chapter 9. Being Sikh in the Modern World

1. Sarawati Kaur Khalsa. "Raising Sikh Children in the Modern World." *Sikhnet.com.* SikhNet, 28 July 2017. Web. 5 Sep. 2017.

2. Eleanor Nesbitt. *Sikhism: A Very Short Introduction.* 2nd ed. Oxford, UK: Oxford UP, 2016. Print. 130.

3. "Global Gender Gap Index 2016." *Weforum.org.* World Economic Forum, 2016. Web. 25 Aug. 2016.

4. Khalsa, "Raising Sikh Children in the Modern World."

5. Gurinder Singh Mann, Paul Numrich, and Raymond Williams. *Buddhists, Hindus, and Sikhs in America.* New York, NY: Oxford UP. 2001. Print. 146.

6. Mann, Numrich, and Williams, *Buddhists, Hindus, and Sikhs,* 146–147.

INDEX

ABOUT THE AUTHOR

Michael Regan worked as a community college and university career counselor before turning his attention to research and writing. He is especially interested in topics related to technology and current events. In his spare time, he enjoys watercolor painting, hiking, tai chi, and reading. He lives in southern Arizona with his spouse and two cats.